D0021500

Presented to:

_____

Presented by:

_____

Date:

_____

I love thee, I love but thee
With a love that shall not die
Till the sun grows cold
And the stars grow old.

WILLIAM SHAKESPEARE

Fun & Creative Dates

for Married Couples

52

Ways to Enjoy Life Together!

HOWARD BOOKS

A DIVISION OF SIMON & SCHUSTER

New York   London   Toronto   Sydney

Published by Howard Books, a division of Simon & Schuster, Inc.
1230 Avenue of the Americas, New York, NY 10020

HOWARD
BOOKS

Fun & Creative Dates for Married Couples—52 Ways to Enjoy Life Together! ©
2008 by Dave Bordon and Associates, LLC

Library of Congress Cataloging-in-Publication Data
Fun & creative dates for married couples : 52 ways to enjoy life together!
    p. cm.
  1. Married people. 2. Dating (Social customs) I. Howard Books. II. Title: Fun
and creative dates for married couples.
  HQ734.F943 2008
  646.7'8—dc22

2008013738

ISBN-13: 978-1-4165-6493-5
ISBN-10:   1-4165-6493-4

10 9 8 7 6 5 4 3

HOWARD and colophon are registered trademarks of Simon & Schuster, Inc.

Manufactured in the United States of America

For information regarding special discounts for bulk purchases, please contact: Simon
& Schuster Special Sales at 1-800-456-6798 or business@simonandschuster.com.

Project developed by Bordon Books, Tulsa, Oklahoma
Project writing and compilation: Christy Phillippe, Shawna McMurry, and Rayné
Bordon in association with Bordon Books; Rebecca Currington in association with
Snapdragon Group℠ Editorial Services
Edited by Chrys Howard
Cover and Interior design by Lori Jackson, LJ Design
Illustrations by Vanda Grigorovic

Introduction

You try to set aside a date night each week. Time just for the two of you; time to rekindle the passion, stoke the embers. Not an easy task these days. You are both so overwhelmed by a schedule that would fluster a politician two weeks before election day. Besides that, the dates—when you get them—have become a little "been there, done that."

If that sounds like you and your spouse, this little book could be the answer to your prayers. Inside, there are fifty-two (one for each week) suggestions for date night. Many are inexpensive or cost nothing at all. Others will require you to plan carefully and put some money away ahead of time. There are fun dates, reflective dates, extreme dates, dates that focus on conversation—all kinds of dates. Each one contains that magical element we call romance.

As you read, may you find just what you need to revitalize your date night—or day—and put the "marvelous" back into your marriage.

Contents

What is Love?

Patience

Kindness

Generosity

Humility

Selflessness

Courtesy

Holiness

Honesty

1. Music Makes the World Go 'Round

Do you love rock and roll, or is jazz more your style? Whatever your musical taste, a concert can be a great place to let loose and enjoy some time together doing something out of the ordinary. If you both enjoy the same types of music, pick an artist or group you both love. If your musical tastes differ, each of you should choose a concert you'd like to go to. If you can, attend both. If not, flip a coin to decide whose pick to go with. Regardless of who wins the coin toss, join in and have fun as if you're the group's biggest fan.

Budget

$$ Prices will vary depending on the location of the seats and the popularity of the artist. For an inexpensive date, look for a free outdoor concert in your area.

Over the Top

Make the evening more memorable by splurging on front row seats or backstage passes.

Get Connected

- If you have a specific artist or group in mind, visit their website for concert information.

- Key search words: concerts, bands followed by your city and state

Life is a flower of which love is the honey.

VICTOR HUGO

2. Old-Fashioned Hayride

Organize an old-fashioned hayride for the two of you—or invite a few other romantically inclined couples to join you. Before you get started, to get yourself in the mood, rake some leaves on a crisp, golden, autumn day. When you've got the biggest pile you can possibly make, hold hands and take a running leap right onto it. Lie down and gaze up at the blue sky and puffy clouds, just as you did when you were kids.

Budget

$$ Relatively inexpensive

What to Take

- Warm clothing

- Blankets

- Fixings to make s'mores

Steps to Success:

Be sure to wear warm, layered clothing that can be added or removed easily as the weather dictates.

Over the Top:

- End the hayride at a bonfire with a great grilled dinner waiting.

- Take along a CD player with your favorite guitar music to enjoy with the bonfire.

 Get Connected:

Key search words: horses, hayride, horse ranch

3. Let's Get Festive

Plan a day-trip to a local or surrounding area "street festival." A lot of these festivals revolve around the produce of that locale such as a grape festival, pecan festival, or watermelon festival. There are usually lots of activities planned around the event including carnivals, fairs, craft shows, and even antique car shows. Of course, the food is the main attraction! If you attend a peach festival, for example, then you are sure to find treats such as peach jam, pies, ice cream, and anything else peach you can imagine. And since most of these festivals occur in quaint, historic towns, you'll be able to explore all their unique sites of interest as well. Did you know there is a town that has the "world's largest rocking chair"? Who knows what you will find! You might even want to stay the weekend!

Budget

$-$$ (just enough for gas and food for the day)

What to Take

- Casual clothes (light jacket for evening, if needed)

- Good walking shoes

- Fun CD for the road

- Camera for all those local points of interest

- Water bottles

Steps to Success

- Be on the road early so you will have the entire day to explore.

- Make sure your car has been serviced (oil change, tire pressure checked, etc.).

Over the Top

- Plan to stay the weekend at a local motel or bed-and-breakfast.

- Buy a neat souvenir to remind you of your trip.

Get Connected

- If the festival has a separate website, check for schedule of events.

- The town hosting the event may also have a site. Look for local areas of interest.

- Key search words: festivals, tourism followed by your state

4. Picnicking Under the Stars

What could be more romantic than a night sky? That's easy: two lovers out under it! For a date that will put stars in your eyes, try the following ideas:

- Picnic under the stars at twilight.

- As the sky deepens, learn the constellations and point them out to each other.

- If you picnic during July or August, you may be able to witness the Perseid meteor shower.

- Look for shooting stars and make wishes on them.

- Contemplate the harvest moon.

- Cuddle in a sleeping bag for two as twilight turns to velvety darkness.

Budget

$ (food for the picnic)

What to Take

- Picnic blanket and supplies

- Warm clothing

- Sleeping bags (or a bag for two)

Steps to Success

- Check the weather.

- Pick a field or meadow outside of town with an unimpeded view of the sky. Be sure it is a safe place.

 **Over the Top:**

- Take a deck of cards or board game and play by flashlight.

- Consider visiting your local planetarium. After the show, go outside and see if you can name the stars or locate a constellation.

- Discuss the universe and our world on the drive home. Watch out—this could lead to an even deeper discussion about the meaning of life.

 Get Connected:

Key search words: Planets, stars, constellations, planetariums, universe

5. Heads Up!

A new spin on the old miniature golf standby is disc golf. It's played with specially designed Frisbees, and most cities have parks that are equipped for this sport. Best of all, after your initial investment in a few discs, it's free to play and can provide

hours of fun in the great outdoors. Discs can be purchased at most sporting goods stores. There are almost as many different kinds of discs as there are golf clubs, but a couple of multipurpose discs and maybe a putter are all you'll need to get started. You don't need to be particularly athletic or coordinated to play. Just have fun. It's a great way to get some exercise and to talk your loved one into going to the park if he or she isn't particularly interested in romantic walks. Keep score if you want, and maybe even agree on a prize for the winner. But don't let the competition overshadow your true goal of spending time together and growing closer. If you're both highly competitive, you may want to agree on a handicap system so each of you has an equal chance of winning.

Budget

$-$$ (if you have to buy a disc)

What to Take

- Disc

- Water bottles

- Running shoes

Steps to Success

Know the rules but don't let them get in the way of fun.

Over the Top

- Pack a romantic picnic lunch including items such as deli meats, cheese, crackers, fruit, and a decadent dessert. Some sparkling grape juice or cider is also a nice addition.

- Visit the park ahead of time and leave some love notes at a few of the holes (nothing too personal since other golfers may see them first!).

Get Connected

- If you are a novice, check out *everythingdisc.com* for rules and beginner disc recommendations.

- There's even a video game version at *miniclip.com/discgolf.htm*.

- Key search words: disc golf followed by your city and state

Romance Her

They say "diamonds are
a girl's best friend," but there is
one thing she will cherish even more
—a love letter from her sweetheart.
Find some pretty paper and simply pour out
your heart. Tell her how much she means to
you and those things you love most
about her. Whether your note is
long or relatively short, you'll
knock the ball out of the park
with this one.

6. Romantic Getaway

Leave your cares behind and sneak away to a bed-and-breakfast for a relaxing weekend of romance. Choose an inn that fits your personalities, whether it be a rustic cabin with a Western feel or an elegant Victorian inn with lots of charm and history. Many bed-and-breakfasts offer spa robes, afternoon tea, whirlpool tubs, and scrumptious desserts. Inquire about specifics when you make the reservation. Make sure to take advantage of every opportunity to be pampered.

Budget

$$-$$$ A stay at a bed-and-breakfast tends to run slightly higher than a night at a hotel, but the quality amenities, gourmet homemade breakfasts, and personal touches far outweigh the slight difference in price.

Over the Top

- Check out the local restaurants and make a reservation for a romantic dinner.

- Plan a longer trip, finding interesting bed-and-breakfast inns to stay in on the way to your destination.

- Take a trip overseas and stay in a bed-and-breakfast or a castle.

Get Connected

- To locate a bed-and-breakfast in the United States, *bbonline.com* is a great site to check. For bed-and-breakfast listings worldwide, try *bnbchoices.com*. Another good site to take a look at is *bedandbreakfast.com*.

- Key search words: bed-and-breakfast, inn, cabins

Where there is great love, there are always miracles.

WILLA CATHER

7. Trip Down Memory Lane

What do you remember most about the day you and your sweetheart first met? How about your first date? For a fun, nostalgic date, see if you can re-create the moment you first met or your first date. See how much you can remember and try to get the details as close to the original as possible. Do you remember what you each were wearing? If you don't have those same clothes anymore, see if you can find something similar. If you went out to eat or to a movie or ball game on your first date, try to arrange to sit in the same seats. Were other friends or family members involved in your meeting? Why not include them in the fun and see if they'd like to help you re-create the moment you met? Whether this date is simple or elaborate, have a great time refreshing your memories of an important milestone in your love story.

Budget

$-$$$ The amount you spend on this date will depend on how elaborate you choose to get or on what you did on your first date. If you've moved away and can't afford the traveling expenses to return to the original location, see if you can find someplace similar nearby.

Over the Top

> Re-create your proposal. To make the event even more special, you could surprise your loved one with a new wedding band or some other piece of jewelry.

 Get Connected

> Go online to check the current status of locations you'd like to revisit, to order tickets to a movie or event, or to find specific items to make your reenactment more authentic.

8. The Great Cookie Hunt

See if you can find the best cookie in your city. Visit local bakeries, the cookie shop at your local mall—anyplace you can think of that makes good cookies. You'll probably want to sample just a bite or two of each cookie, and then take the rest home to enjoy later so you don't end your date early with an upset stomach! If you can't agree on just one winner, you could each rank them from your favorite to least favorite and see which cookie shows up towards the top of each of your lists. This activity could be especially fun during the

Christmas season, when there will be additional holiday selections to choose from; and you just may find the perfect treat to take to holiday parties.

Budget

$ Cookies are usually a fairly inexpensive treat.

Over the Top

- See if you can come up with your own original cookie recipe and give it a sentimental name that has something to do with your love story.

- Spend the evening baking your recipe together.

Get Connected

Key search words: bakeries, cookies, cookie recipes

Who has not found the heaven below

Will fail of it above.

God's residence is next to mine,

His furniture is love.

Emily Dickinson

9. Test-Drive Your Dream Car

When you hear the words *dream car*, what image springs to mind? If it's the latest minivan with the perfect setup for your growing family, try thinking a little further—beyond what's practical to something

that's just plain fun. What about the shiny sports car he's dreamed of driving since he was a little boy? Or maybe the snazzy convertible she pictured herself in during her single days. Decide what it is you're looking for, and then head to the car lot for a test-drive. Even if your dream car is destined to remain in the realm of fantasy, you can still have a great time checking out the car lots and sharing your dream with each other.

 **Budget**

$ A test drive won't cost you anything, but if you're prone to impulse buying, you may want to leave your checkbook and credit cards at home!

 **Over the Top**

- Rent your dream car for the weekend and take it on a road trip, or rent it when you get to your destination and have a blast driving it around town.

- If your dream car is something you'd both honestly like to own someday, why not set up a separate savings account and start working toward that goal a little at a time?

 Get Connected

- Get online to find a dealership in your area that carries your dream car.

- Most of the major auto manufacturers have websites where you can "build" a customized version of your dream car online.

- Key search words: dream car, dream car rentals

Grow Old Along with Me

Grow old along with me!

The best is yet to be.

The last of life, for which the first
was made;

Our times are in his hand,

Who saith, "A whole I planned,

Youth shows but half; trust God:

See all, nor be afraid!"

ROBERT BROWNING

10. Lazy Day

Sometimes the best plan is no plan at all. If you're weary of having to stick to schedules and agendas, maybe a lazy day at home is in order. Spend the day in your pajamas. Do crossword puzzles together, read the paper or a book to each other, or watch your favorite movie. If it's nice out, swing in a hammock together and sip some lemonade. One glass, two straws. Order in dinner. Do whatever helps you relax—those simple pleasures that a busy schedule rarely allows.

 **Budget**

$ If you're like most people, you probably have plenty of unused lazy-day activities around the house, so your only expense should be food.

 **Over the Top**

- Call a local spa and order "at home" massages for two. Now that's relaxing!

- To remove yourself completely from the temptation to do anything but relax, rent a cabin in the woods for the weekend and spend a lazy weekend enjoying the beauty and solitude of nature.

 **Get Connected**

Key search words: crosswords, cabin rentals

11. Renovating the Nest

For a fun and memorable day that will have a lasting reward, try tackling a small project around the house together. Keep it simple, fun, and romantic—something that's not too difficult and not already on a "to do" list. You could install a porch swing or add a splash of color and some decorative touches to your bedroom. Or, if you're handy at woodworking, you could try something a little bigger, like building a gazebo in the backyard. Make it something you can enjoy together, and be sure to pick a project that won't raise your stress level if you aren't able to finish it as quickly as planned. Have fun working together, but take some breaks and relax together too. If you don't finish in one day or one weekend, you'll have your next date already planned! In the end, you'll have something you'll enjoy for years to come, and you can be proud to tell others you did it yourselves.

 **Budget**

$-$$$ Your budget will depend largely on what project you choose and how many of the necessary tools you already own.

What to Take

- Any necessary tools or supplies

- Wear old clothes. After all, you never know when a paint or water fight might break out!

Steps to Success

- Remember that your main goal is to have fun together.

- If you make a mistake, laugh about it together. Sometimes it's the imperfections that give a piece its character.

Over the Top

Build a natural habitat in your yard to attract wildlife such as birds and butterflies and beneficial insects.

Get Connected

Both *hgtv.com* and *design.discovery.com* have great project ideas.

Love spends his all, and still hath store.

P. J. BAILEY

12. Finger Foods Only

Prepare a meal made up entirely of finger foods, and have fun feeding each other. Menu selections could include shrimp cocktail, petite quiches, crackers, cheese cubes, grapes, fresh cherries, petit fours, and chocolate-covered strawberries. If you have a fireplace, you could even prepare some small kabobs and cook them over the fire, followed by roasted marshmallows or s'mores for dessert. Another fun and romantic variation would be to feed each other fondue. Be creative!

Set the scene for your dinner with dim lighting, candles, and romantic music. You may want to spread a blanket on the floor and eat picnic style or place your food on a tray and snuggle up on the sofa.

Budget

$-$$ Of course, you may get quite elaborate with your menu if you wish, but simple fare can be just as enjoyable.

Over the Top

If you don't already have one, purchase an outdoor fire pit or chiminea for your backyard. Either prepare your dinner over it or feed each other by the light of it. Take some blankets or sleeping bags out with you so you can snuggle up and stargaze after you're finished.

Get Connected

Key search words: recipes, finger food recipes, fondue

Love is a canvas furnished by nature and embroidered by imagination.

VOLTAIRE

13. Window-Shopping

If you're looking for something to do but don't want to spend a lot of money, visit your local mall or an upscale shopping area and do some window-shopping. Check out the latest electronic gadgets. Get ideas for decorating your home. Visit the toy store and have fun playing with the display items. Take some goofy photos together in a photo booth.

Treat yourselves to lunch at a restaurant you've never tried before. And be sure to keep your eyes and ears open; after all, this is the perfect opportunity to get gift ideas for your sweetheart for future occasions.

 **Budget**

> $-$$ Window-shopping doesn't cost a thing, but you will want to plan to spend a little for lunch and anything you might find to do along the way. You could also plan a small amount to spend on a just-for-fun purchase.

 **Steps to Success**

> - Remember that the reason you're there is to have fun together, so avoid the temptation to "bargain shop" unless it's for something you're both excited about.

- Try to divide your time equally between things he's interested in and things she wants to look at. If you stop in a clothing store for her, make your next stop a music store or something else of his choice.

 **Over the Top**

Visit the Mall of America in Minnesota. In addition to over 500 stores, it houses an amusement park, an aquarium, a fourteen-screen movie theater, and many other attractions.

 Get Connected

- For information about the Mall of America, visit *mallofamerica.com*.

- Key search words: shopping, shopping malls followed by your city and state

Romance Him

Tell your florist you want
to send your husband flowers at
the office. Women send men flowers
all the time these days, and your florist will
know just how to arrange and package
them for maximum masculine appeal.
He might act a little embarrassed
at first, but he won't be able to
hide the smile. Don't forget to
attach a romantic note.

14. Weekend in the Great Outdoors

For a fun weekend getaway, pack up the tent and sleeping bags and head to a nearby state or national park. Enjoy hiking and exploring the area, and keep a close eye out for wildlife. An early-morning hike will often provide the best opportunity to spot unusual birds and other animals. A night-time hike can be exciting too, but make sure you take a flashlight and stay on marked paths close to the campground. If there is a lake or stream nearby, be sure to take a swimsuit so you can cool off with an afternoon swim. You may even want to consider renting a canoe or paddleboat while you're there to do some floating. When you return to your campsite after a full day of adventure, enjoy relaxing by a warm campfire and roasting hot dogs and marshmallows under the stars.

Budget

$-$$ If you already have camping gear, this date should be quite reasonable. Most parks charge a small fee for your campsite.

What to Take

- Comfortable clothing and shoes for hiking. If it is summer, don't forget swimwear.

- Your camping gear, including a tent, sleeping bags or an air mattress, pillows, a lantern, flashlight, toiletries, bug repellent, and sunscreen

- Firewood or an ax or saw for collecting wood

- A cooler stocked with food, water, and other beverages

Over the Top

- Camp on the beach.

- Many parks offer hike-in campsites. These sites are more secluded, but they usually don't have bathroom facilities nearby.

- Take a trip to the Grand Canyon. Hike to the bottom with your gear in tow, and stay the night at a campground there. This adventure is for experienced and well-conditioned hikers only.

 **Get Connected**

- You can find listings of national parks at *nps.gov.*

- Key search words: the name of your state followed by the words state parks, camping, hiking, camping checklist

Letters are those winged messengers that fly from east to west on embassies of love.

JEREMIAH BROWN HOWELL

15. Say Cheese!

If you've been married for a while, or especially
if you have kids, it's probably been awhile since
you've had a picture taken of just the two of you.
Why not have a portrait made? You could dress
nicely and go with a traditional pose, or you could
do something off the wall—something that dem-
onstrates your individual personalities. If you're
into sports, you could wear your fan gear for the
picture. You could dress in Western wear or in
period clothing from an era you've always been
intrigued by. Wear crazy hats or include something

more subtle in the picture, like a small finger puppet peeking out of one of your pockets. Have fun and be creative, and allow your photographer creative license as well.

Another fun variation of this idea is to have your caricature drawn. You may be able to find a caricaturist doing drawings at your local mall, an amusement park, or in an entertainment district

of town on weekends. Whether you decide on a portrait or caricature, you'll have a fun memento to enjoy for years to come.

$ Budget

$-$$ Cost will depend upon what studio you go to and how many pictures you purchase. Be sure to check the studio's website before you go for current special offers. Caricatures are usually fairly inexpensive.

WOW Over the Top

- Take an art class together, and attempt drawing portraits of each other.

- Have an artist draw, paint, or sculpt a portrait of the two of you. If you really want to go "over the top," have this done on the streets of New Orleans, New York, or even Paris.

Get Connected

Key search words: portraits, caricatures, caricaturists followed by your city and state

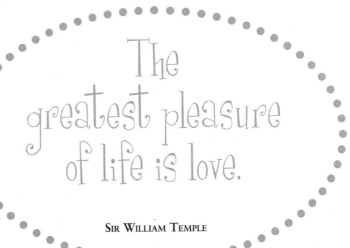

The greatest pleasure of life is love.

Sir William Temple

16. Lights, Camera, Action!

Ever wanted to try your hand at directing or
acting? How about doing your own short feature
film re-creating your own love story?

You can make this as simple or as elaborate as
you wish. Return to your special places and take
turns describing on video how you felt back then
and now, and include all the details. What did
you notice first about each other? What unusual
circumstances brought you together? Who did most
of the talking in the early stages of the relationship?

Or, put some time and thought into it by writing your own script and brainstorming about all the shots you want to take. There is such a thing as literary license so you can embellish the details to make it more interesting, or you could even make it into a romantic comedy. Of course, if you are both realists, you can stick to the original.

However you choose to tell your story, this activity will provide a date filled with fun and sentimentality. It will also create something you will cherish for years to come.

Budget

$$-$$$ You'll need to rent or purchase video equipment. Software is also available to edit your video.

What to Take

Wedding pictures to be incorporated into the film.

Over the Top

Hire someone to do filming and editing for a truly "big" production!

Get Connected

Key search words: writing a movie script, editing your own movie

17. Romantic Rendezvous

Enjoy the anticipation and excitement of a first date all over again. Take separate cars and agree to meet at a bookstore or coffee shop at a certain time. When you arrive, flirt with each other as if you were strangers meeting for the first time. Ask each other

questions as if you were just getting acquainted. Be truthful with your answers or get creative, developing a whole new persona that you could imagine yourself as. Agree on a time and place for a "second date," or leave together and let the evening take you where it will.

 **Budget**

$-$$ This date could be kept as simple as conversation over a cup of coffee or it could continue on to dinner and dancing or a movie.

 **Over the Top**

- Send your loved one flowers at work with a note attached that indicates when and where he or she should meet you later. Sign the note "your secret admirer." (In order to avoid any confusion, you may want to include some kind of clue only your spouse would understand to indicate that the "secret admirer" is really you.)

• If time allows, build the anticipation by placing clues and/or small gifts at several locations around town, each leading to the next spot until he or she finally reaches the destination where you'll meet.

 Get Connected

Key search words: first date, conversation starters

How Many Times

How many times do I love again?
Tell me how many beads there are
In a silver chain of evening rain
Unravelled from the trembling main
And threading the eye of a yellow star—
So many times do I love again.

THOMAS LOVELL BEDDOES

18. Bicycle Built for Two

Have fun trying something new together and get a good workout at the same time. Find a bicycle shop that has rentals and rent a tandem bicycle for the day. Take it for a leisurely ride along a scenic trail or ride it around an area with shops and other points of interest where you could stop to take breaks along the way. You may wish to take a picnic lunch along with you, or you could stop at an outdoor café for lunch. Ask a passerby to take a picture of the two of you on the bike to commemorate the experience.

Budget

$$ Your main expense will be the bike rental. You may also need to purchase or rent helmets if you don't already own some.

What to Take

- Water bottles

- Sunscreen and sunglasses

- Bicycle helmets

Over the Top

- Take a guided tandem bicycle tour of Ireland or some other location that offers these unique experiences.

- If you find this is something you really enjoy, consider purchasing your own tandem bicycle.

- Enter a tandem bike race and enjoy training and working toward a goal together.

 Get Connected

Key search words: tandem cycling, tandem tours, bike rentals

All that we love deeply becomes a part of us.

HELEN KELLER

19. Romantic Movie Night

Turn an ordinary movie rental into a memorable private viewing event created just for the two of you. Set up a fancy candlelight dinner in view of the television so you can dine in style as you watch the movie. Or set up a luxurious seating area with plenty of pillows and blankets for snuggling, either on the floor or sofa. Add special touches with flowers and other decorations throughout the room. Get dressed up for the event as if you were attending an exclusive viewing party.

Budget

$-$$ Movie rentals are inexpensive. Other expenses may include dinner, flowers, and decorations.

Over the Top

- Some museums and community centers offer outdoor viewings of classic movies. See if you can find one of these special events in your area.

- Surprise your spouse by having a surround-sound theater system installed just before your special movie night.

- Take a sleeping bag and portable DVD player to the backyard and watch your movie under the stars.

Get Connected

Key search words: movie rentals, romantic movies, movie on the lawn

No cord nor
cable can so forcibly draw,
or hold so fast, as love can do
with a twined thread.

ROBERT BURTON

20. Shall We Dance?

Was your wedding day the last time you stepped foot on a dance floor? If so, maybe it's time to dust off your dancing shoes and take a whirl around the floor with your sweetheart. What kind of dancing do you enjoy? There are many styles to choose from—ballroom, line dancing, the two-step, swing, salsa—the list goes on and on. If you're new to dance, watch an instructional DVD or take lessons before you go out on your own. Even if you can hold your own on the dance floor, try a new style you've never attempted before. You'll have fun learning something new together, and dancing is a great way to stay in shape as well. If you have trouble finding a place to show off your new moves, check with local dance studios that teach couples' classes. Many of them host open dances or will have some suggestions on where to go dancing.

 Budget

$-$$$ Prices will vary depending on whether you choose to take lessons or purchase a DVD and teach yourselves.

Over the Top

Create your own private dance floor on a patio or in a room with wood or tile floors. Decorate with items such as flowers, candles, tulle, and white Christmas lights. Prepare a CD ahead of time with a mix of your favorite romantic songs that will fit the dance styles you've been practicing. Get dressed up for the occasion as if you were going out. If you wish, start your evening with a white tablecloth, candlelight dinner, and then dance the night away.

Key search words: ballroom dancing,
country dancing, salsa dancing, swing
dance, dance DVDs, dance instruction

My bounty is as boundless as the sea,

My love as deep; the more I give to thee,

The more I have, for both are infinite.

WILLIAM SHAKESPEARE

21. Become Art Critics

Tap into a plethora of great date activities by familiarizing yourself with your city's performing arts scene. Check your local newspaper or other local periodicals, as well as your city's website, for information about upcoming events. Attend a play or musical production put on by a community theater group. See if there is a Shakespeare in the Park organization in your area. Visit an area coffee shop on a night when they are hosting a live musical performance by a local artist. At Christmastime, attend a local production of Handel's *Messiah*,

Dickens' *A Christmas Carol*, or Tchaikovsky's *The Nutcracker*. Check area churches and colleges for productions you might enjoy attending. While local performances may not always be as polished as a performance by a professional company, they are usually much more affordable, allowing you to attend more events; and you can feel good about supporting local artists and perhaps helping them to get their start.

Budget

> $-$$ If you watch for them, you can probably find many events in your area that are free of charge.

What to Take

- Camera, just in case there is a photo opportunity with the cast

- Binoculars, if you don't have perfect seats

Over the Top

- Purchase season passes to your local performing arts center or for a company or theater group you particularly enjoy.

- Join a community theater group and experience firsthand the thrill of performing.

Get Connected

- Check the website of your city or your city's arts council for a calendar of events.

- Key search words: community theater, performing arts center, opera, ballet, local artists followed by your city and state

Romance
is the glamour which
turns the dust of everyday
life into a golden haze.

ELINOR GLYN

22. Blast from the Past

There's nothing like a visit to your hometown to bring back treasured memories of your childhood and adolescence. If you both grew up in the same town, you'll probably have lots of shared memories to enjoy. If not, double your fun by visiting both of your hometowns and showing each other around. Drive by your elementary school and high school. Take a walk through your old neighborhood and visit the house where you grew up. Have a picnic at the park or playground where you used to play. Even if you've been married for years, you may be surprised at the things you can learn about each other by taking such a trip.

Budget

$$-$$$ You'll need to plan to take enough money for transportation, food, and accommodations, as well as a little extra for any events, activities, or shopping you find to do while you're there.

What to Take

- Be sure to take along some baby and childhood photos and high school yearbooks to add to your experience and help jog your memory.

- Remember your camera so you can take pictures of the town as it is now to commemorate your return visit and to compare to old photos later.

 **Over the Top**

- Visit your high school on a school day and see how much things have changed.

- Go to a high school football game or other community event while you're there.

- Plan your visit around a special event in the town, like a fall festival or anniversary celebration.

- Rent some bikes and pedal your way around town.

- Contact the current owner of your child-hood home to see if they'll allow you to take a tour. It never hurts to ask!

 **Get Connected**

See if your hometown has a website and check it for a list of events to help you plan your itinerary.

Romance
Her

Leave a pink index card
where she will find it and instruct
her to follow the clues for a pleasant
surprise. On the back of the card, give
her the first clue that sends her to the location
of the next clue, and the next, and the next,
until she finds her way to where you
are waiting with a kiss and flowers
or a small gift.

23. Create a Masterpiece

Explore your creative side with a fun, lighthearted art project. Get out some finger paints and a large piece of paper and see what you can create together. You could agree to do a picture of something in particular or go completely abstract. Or you could pick up a paint-by-number picture and have fun working on the design together. While you're waiting for your masterpiece to dry, go to the store and find the perfect frame to display your work so you can preserve this special memento of the fun you have as a couple.

Budget

$ The art supplies for these projects are inexpensive; and, if you have kids, you may already have these supplies around the house. You can even make your own finger paints. Recipes are available online.

Over the Top

- Take an art class together. There are lots of options—oil painting, watercolor, pottery, mosaics, and many others.

- Visit an art museum for inspiration. Some museums will even allow you to take your art supplies along and work on your project on the museum grounds.

- Eat at a restaurant that displays local talent.

Key search words: finger paints, paint by
number, art classes, art museums

The little
unremembered acts of
kindness and love are the
best parts of a
person's life.

WILLIAM WORDSWORTH

24. See the Lights Sparkle

What better time to stoke the embers of romance in your marriage than at Christmastime? Houses and city streets are all aglow with lights and cheerful tidings. Perhaps there is a glistening blanket of

snow on the ground, making everything new once again. Make the most of this magical time of year by bundling up, grabbing a mug of steaming hot cocoa, and heading outside for a romantic walk through a winter wonderland. You could walk around your own neighborhood to admire your neighbors' Christmas lights, or you could find a particularly beautiful area of town to stroll through. Many churches, parks, and even zoos go all out with Christmas displays you can enjoy. Many museums even have special Christmas festivities like gingerbread house displays and a "festival of trees" event.

Budget

$ Most Christmas light displays are free to look at. A few places may charge a small admission fee.

 Over the Top

Take a trolley, helicopter, or limousine ride to see the Christmas lights.

Get Connected

Key search words: Christmas displays, Christmas lights, zoo, trolley, helicopter rides, limousine rentals, festival of trees

25. Lend a Hand

There is, perhaps, nothing that will draw you closer to each other than to reach out to others as a couple through volunteer work. There are opportunities to suit any personality and set of skills or talents. Volunteer to help build houses for low-income families through Habitat for Humanity. Join a team to help beautify local parks or plant trees around town. Coach your child's ball team together. Teach a Sunday school class as a team or host a small group fellowship in your home. Make deliveries for Meals on Wheels or serve breakfast at the Salvation Army. You could even don a clown costume and some makeup or learn to juggle or do magic tricks and entertain sick children at the hospital. Whatever areas you may be gifted in, using those talents to touch the lives and hearts of others will strengthen the bond between the two of you and will give you even more reasons to admire each other.

Budget

$ The only thing most of these activities will cost you is your time and effort, and the rewards are priceless.

 **Over the Top**

- Go on a mission trip together to another country. The shared experience will bless the lives of others and could very well change your lives as well.

- Try using your pet for "pet therapy." Many cities have organizations that take pets into hospitals and nursing homes. This will require training and usually certification.

 Get Connected

- Check out these "pet therapy" websites: *deltasociety.org*, *peopleanimalslove.org*.

- Key search words: volunteer opportunities followed by your city and state, Habitat for Humanity, clowning, Salvation Army, Meals on Wheels, pet therapy

26. Extreme Adventure

Is there something extreme you've always wanted to try but haven't quite mustered up the courage to do yet? Combine your bravery and tackle it

together. Go bungee jumping, skydiving, or hang gliding. Go on a heli-hike, an outdoor adventure in which you're taken to a drop-off spot by helicopter and must hike your way back to the pick-up location. Take a whitewater rafting trip. Whatever your extreme ambition might be, take it on together and create a memory you'll tell others about for years to come.

Budget

$$-$$$ Some of these adventures can be quite pricey, but keep in mind that it's a once-in-a-lifetime experience and a memory that will last forever.

Over the Top

- Backpack your way through Europe, staying in hostels along the way.

- Go on an African safari or other extreme adventure tour.

- Dog fight in a real fighter plane or take a race car for a spin on a super speedway. (Nascar offers racing schools at selected speedways with instruction and actual driving time in a race car.)

Get Connected

Key search words: bungee jumping, sky-diving, hang gliding, heli-hike, whitewater rafting, extreme adventures, fly in a fighter jet, drive a race car, rock climbing

Romance
Him

Whether or not he enjoys
poetry, a poem written by you
telling of your love for him is a
beautiful gift. Then have it framed as a
keepsake of your abiding love. The poem does
not have to be perfect in rhyme or meter.
What he will cherish is the memory
of the time, thought, and love
that went into the writing
of the poem.

27. Let's Build Something

Visit a hobby shop and pick out something you can enjoy building together like a model car, an airplane, or perhaps an interesting puzzle. Try something simple that can be completed in an evening or a more complex, ongoing project that you can add to at your leisure, such as a dollhouse or model train set. When you're finished, keep it as a sentimental memento or give it as a special gift to a friend or family member who would enjoy it. You could even save it as a future gift for your child when he or she is old enough to take care of it.

Budget

$-$$ You should be able to find a project to suit any budget.

Steps to Success

- Read the directions on the box carefully and make sure you have all the necessary supplies before you get started.

- Play some fun music in the background to keep you energized and having fun.

- Don't allow any perfectionist tendencies to get in the way of your having a good time together.

Over the Top

- Enter your completed creation in the county or state fair or some other contest.

- Sign up for a class at your local university or hobby store.

Get Connected

Key search words: hobby shop, craft stores, model airplanes, model cars, dollhouses, model train sets, county/state fair entry rules

> To love
> is to find pleasure in
> the happiness of the
> person loved.
>
> LEIBNITZ

28. Get Historical

For a fun and interesting outing that can be educational too, visit a museum or other local historical landmark. Before you go, arm yourself with information from the Internet so you can make the most of your visit. Talk about items and facts that are particularly interesting to you and about how your perception of history may have differed from reality. Share how the history you're learning may relate to your family's history. You may want to check the museum's calendar of events and plan your visit around a special exhibit, event, or historical reenactment.

Budget

$ Some museums charge a nominal entry fee, while others rely on donations.

Over the Top

- Take a road trip following a historic highway or pioneer trail. Make lots of stops along the way to explore the history of the area.

- Participate as actors in a historical reenactment.

- Visit the Mall and Smithsonian in Washington D.C. and immerse yourself in U.S. history.

- Many states also have whimsical landmarks. For example, Kansas boasts of having the nation's largest sunflower. Make it an ongoing goal to visit as many state landmarks as you can. Have a designated photo album for all your adventures.

Get Connected

- For whacky landmarks, check out *roadsideamerica.com* or Google unusual landmarks followed by the state you are interested in.

- Key search words: national or historical landmarks, museums, historic highways, pioneer trails, or historical reenactment followed by specific state, Smithsonian

29. Backyard Camping

Gather up your tent and some sleeping bags and camp out under the stars in your own backyard. Take turns telling favorite stories or reading suspenseful short stories to each other. Take a star chart with you and try to find some of the constellations. Watch for shooting stars. Catch fireflies. Listen closely to the night sounds and see if you can identify any of the wildlife living just outside your door. Roast hot dogs and marshmallows over your grill. If either of you plays the guitar, take it out with you and sing some campfire songs.

The great thing about this type of camping trip is that there's very little preparation involved. If you forget something, you can just run back inside to get it. And you're guaranteed a clean bathroom and a hot shower in the morning!

Budget

$ If you already have some camping gear, your only expenses will be some hot dogs, buns, and marshmallows for roasting and some citronella candles or bug repellent.

Over the Top

Install or purchase a fire pit to make the experience more realistic.

Get Connected

Key search words: campfire stories, campfire songs, fire pits, star chart

Many waters cannot quench love; rivers cannot wash it away. . . .

SONG OF SONGS 8:7

The White Rose

The red rose whispers of passion,

And the white rose breathes of love;

O, the red rose is a falcon,

And the white rose is a dove.

But I send you a cream-white rosebud

With a flush on its petal tips;

For the love that is purest and sweetest

Has a kiss of desire on the lips.

JOHN BOYLE O'REILLY

30. Progressive Dinner for Two

What you have in mind is something fun, yet romantic, and it includes a night out for dinner. But it's so difficult to decide where to go. You love the artichoke dip at that little place in town—but you'd also like a good steak, and for that you'll probably

want the steakhouse south of town. What about dessert? Your favorite coffeehouse always has the most decadent one, but they don't serve dinner. So what will you do?

How about going to all those places—in one spectacular evening of favorite food and special places?

Drive on over to the place with the yummy artichoke dip and enjoy a great appetizer. They make it just like you like it. Then head to the steakhouse for your entrée—the main course cooked just right. For dessert, move on to the place that offers the best carrot cake in town or a bubbling fruit cobbler. It's your call.

Budget

$$$ The cost of a nice dinner out.

Steps to Success

- Map out your course ahead of time and call each place for reservations if needed.

- Start with your appetizer as early as 4:30 or 5:00 so you will have the time to leisurely enjoy all courses.

- Stick to the plan. Don't talk yourself out of any of the stops on your schedule.

- Remember to tip at each stop.

Over the Top

- Between dinner and dessert, go dancing. It's a great way to work off those calories, and it's a romantic interlude in your evening.

- Plan to spend the night in a nice hotel and order dessert to be shared in your room.

- End the evening with a candlelight dessert back home, where you can linger over it as long as you like.

Get Connected

Check out the menus of your favorite restaurants online.

31. Let's Do It Again!

Just like your original wedding day, the day you renew your vows can also be a very special time for you and your spouse as well as a date you can share (at least to some degree) with others. It can be as upscale or low-key as you desire. You may even want to return to the place where you were married to create that very special event. But it's also fun to indulge yourself in a completely different experience. If you were married in a church, renew your vows in a park or on the beach. How about on a cruise ship at sea? If you chose an informal setting before, opt for a more formal one this time. The pleasure is all yours!

Write out your vows beforehand, but remember, this is a renewal, an affirmation rather than a remarriage. Your vows can be whatever you want them to be. And you won't need a preacher, a blood test, or a marriage license—just yourself and your beloved.

Budget

$$$ The cost will largely depend on whether you go simple or extravagant. You may want to save up for a major anniversary—like your twenty-fifth or fortieth. Or for a more

personal date, set aside only enough for a night on the town and a sleepover at a nice hotel.

 ## What to Take

- For a big affair, you will need a dress, a tux, music, cake, flowers, etc.

- For a smaller, more intimate affair, all you need is an overnight bag and a destination.

Over the Top

For an even greater thrill, plan to renew your vows in an exotic location you've always wanted to visit.

Get Connected

- Check out *Idotaketwo.com* for vow renewal etiquette.

- Key search words: renew wedding vows, honeymoon packages, vacation deals

Let me give
you my heart;
May it only love you.

ANONYMOUS

32. Plant a Vegetable Garden

There's just something about getting your hands dirty, bringing something good from the ground. And gardening together can be a rewarding date you will want to indulge in year after year. A big garden can be a lot of work, but gardens come in all sizes. A planter box is all you need for a date to remember. You can buy a planter box or build one if you have the skills. Or, if you want to do something on a smaller scale, try planting some fresh herbs in some colorful pots on your windowsill. From the planting to the harvest, you'll grow closer

as you grow something together. And partaking of
the finished product will be an extra reward.

Budget

$$ If you have a plot of land that is suitable
for gardening, you won't have much
cost—just some gardening tools, gloves, and
seeds or plants. A planter box will require a
moderate investment, but remember, it can
be used year after year.

Steps to Success

- Gloves are essential in order to prevent
insect bites and small injuries from thorns
and stones.

- Visit a local nursery to find plants suited
for your area.

- Find out how much sun your vegetables

will need and place your planter box wisely.

- You will want to use pesticides only when absolutely necessary.

- See that your garden is out of reach of animals like raccoons, deer, etc.

Get Connected:

Key search words: vegetable garden, planter box, growing herbs

33. Murder Mystery Weekend

Up for a little danger? A murder mystery date is just what you need. You'll experience over-the-top drama as you and your spouse try to gain insight into the identities of the other guests, collect clues, and work together to solve the murder at hand. Such a weekend is a perfect getaway with fun at the top of the menu. These weekends typically are staged in old, restored homes with vintage furnishings, many with reputations for past crimes. Weekends begin on Friday evening with dinner and interactive entertainment and the drama is ongoing until the mystery is solved, usually on Sunday. If an entire weekend is too daunting, Murder Mystery Dinners are also available. The drama for these is a little more intense and the plots more compact, but they provide just as much fun as the longer versions.

Budget

$$$ Weekends include meals and lodging—along with your murder mystery entertainment. You will also have travel expenses unless you can find such an establishment in your area.

Over the Top

Host your own murder mystery dinner or weekend.

Get Connected

- A travel agent can book a murder mystery weekend for you. Google travel agent followed by your city and state.

- Key search words: murder mystery weekend, murder mystery dinner followed by your city and state, hosting a murder mystery dinner

Romance Her

Invite your wife to take a
long, late afternoon walk with you.
Hold her hand and entwine your fingers.
Discuss the beauty around you—green lawns,
blooming flowers, fall leaves, a lake in the
distance, a gently rolling hillside. Then tell
her that her face is the most beautiful
thing you have ever seen and you
would rather look at her than
the most captivating
landscape.

34. Day at the Beach

If you're fortunate enough to live near the beach, you are blessed. You know how fabulous it can be to feel the ocean breezes on your skin and the sand between your toes, listen to the surf, and watch

the waves roll in. You can have all that even if you choose not to get into the cool, refreshing water and feel the waves circulating around your body. There is simply nothing more stimulating than the pungent smell of the ocean and the view you'll see as you throw your towels down on the warm, glistening sand. It's a fabulous date.

If you don't live near the ocean, you have options. Most lakes have sandy beaches and swimming areas—sans salt. Rivers can also provide a refreshing swim and the warm, earthy, exotic smell of a river can be quite wonderful as well.

Even when it's too cold to swim, try walking along the beach together. Even if you don't say a word, you'll have a renewed sense of connectedness.

 Budget

$-$$ Some beaches do charge a small fee, but many are free.

 **What to Take**

- Beach towels

- Sunscreen and sunglasses (glare off the water can be intense)

- Bottled water and beverages (it's easy to become dehydrated in the direct sunlight)

- A sand bucket and two shovels for sculpting sand castles

 **Over the Top**

- Reserve a room in a hotel right on the beach and spend a weekend kicking back with the sand and the surf.

- Go parasailing or horseback riding along the beach.

 Get Connected

Key search words: sculpting sand castles, beachfront hotels

35. Backyard Paradise

Maybe you don't have enough saved for a Caribbean cruise or a weekend in Fiji, but you can still combine romance with water for a great date. On one of those truly wonderful lazy days of summer, hook the hose up to the sprinkler, don your bathing suits, whip up a couple of tropical smoothies—ah, paradise! Place the sprinkler just close enough to your chairs to provide a gentle misting. If, after

a time of sunny relaxation, you feel like getting up and frolicking in the surf, all you need is a little imagination, and you're chasing each other through the spray.

 **Budget**

> $ The cost of mangos, oranges, bananas— and a slightly higher water bill!

 What to Take

- Chaise lounges are best—those wonderful foldout lawn beauties and a beach umbrella

- Sunscreen

- Bright beach towels

- A blender, fruit, and straws for the

smoothies (Toothpick umbrellas are also a nice touch.)

Over the Top

- Plan a wonderful tropical lunch. Consider some of these menu suggestions: Barbeque or jerk chicken (jerk marinade can be found in the salad dressing aisle), chicken salad, pulled pork sandwich, steamed shrimp, oysters, crab dip, and tropical punch.

- Buy some kids' water toys like a water-slide, water guns, and even a kiddie pool and really have fun. Make sure to have a water fight!

Get Connected:

Key search words: backyard water toys, smoothie recipes

36. The Way We Were

What better way to stir the embers of romance than by watching the video of your big day. Most couples say they missed a lot of the actual event due to stress, nerves, and timing, so it's great to sit back together, snuggle up, and relive those few spectacular hours.

When it's just the two of you, you can afford to be completely self-absorbed, whispering your secret thoughts and feelings about that day.

You can also discuss with abandon the whacky outfit Aunt Daisy wore, the soloist who muffed the words of your favorite song, the unfortunate incident at the reception involving your cousin and the wedding cake, and how good you felt when it was all over and you were speeding away from the church in your limo.

This date is guaranteed to have you laughing, crying, and falling in love all over again.

 **Budget**

> $ Most photography packages now include a wedding video. If yours did, you've already paid for this date. If you don't have a video, get out your wedding album and start flipping the pages. Different format—same memories!

# Over the Top

- For a really special evening, dress up to watch your video. Pull out your wedding gown and rent a tuxedo.

- Reserve a suite at a luxurious hotel in your area and arrive by limo. Enjoy a candlelight dinner in your room, and then watch your video together. Almost all hotel rooms have VCR and DVD players, but be sure to ask ahead of time.

- If you don't have a wedding DVD, have your special photos put into a slideshow and set to your favorite music.

Get Connected

Key search words: romantic hotel package followed by your city and state, DVD slideshow software

37. The Family Tree

Ever wonder if you or your spouse might have a pirate or an outlaw in your ancestral line? Wouldn't it be fun to find out? Even if your ancestry happens to be tame, it is always interesting to discover your roots. Begin by listing all the family members you can remember. You can do this at a restaurant or coffeehouse. Take along a poster board, permanent markers, and family pictures. Tell each other stories and describe all the characters that make you who you are. Now is the time to reveal any secrets you may have forgotten to tell your spouse about that long-lost uncle. Remember, no judging. As you are laughing and learning about each other's families, you will also be creating a wonderful pass-me-down gift for your children.

 Budget

$-$$ This is a priceless date with a small price tag, depending on where you go. If you choose to do this at home, choose a comfortable place and make some snacks for nibbling. (If you have kids, be sure to hire a sitter.)

 What to Take

Collect photos and stories from your family.

Over the Top

- Buy family tree software and manage your information on your computer.

- Spend a day with one of your oldest relatives. Record their stories on video to keep for posterity.

Get Connected

- To explore more of your genealogies, try *familysearch.com* or *familytree.com*.

- Check out *myheritage.com* for a free site that allows you to input information and then builds the family tree for you.

You Complete Me

He is the half part of a blessed man

Left to be finished by such as she;

And she is fair divided excellence,

Whole fullness of perfection lies in him.

O, two such silver current, when they join,

Do glorify the banks that found them in!

GEOFFREY CHAUCER

38. Enjoy High Tea

There's a reason the British are so devoted to their daily teatime. It's fun. It's relaxing. And it provides a great way to put the day in perspective. Why not grab your spouse by the hand and give it a try?

Afternoon tea began in the mid-1700s and was used by the British working class to ward off hunger before dinner. Today, it is an elegant affair served in hotels and restaurants around the world. In such a setting, it will likely include tea sandwiches, puddings, cakes, crumpets, and scones, served with jellies, marmalades, and fruit spreads, as well as a variety of hot teas. This is a great date when you want to spend time just relaxing together and enjoying stress-free conversation.

If you don't feel like going out for tea, try taking a break from your weekend chores to enjoy a mid-afternoon date at the kitchen table.

 **Budget**

$$-$$$ High tea at a fancy hotel will be expensive, but many towns now have small teahouses that are reasonable. If you choose to have tea at home, you can still make it fancy without great expense.

 **What to Take**

- Teapot or tea set

- Your best china and linens

- Tearoom foods

 **Over the Top**

Stay at a local bed-and-breakfast for the weekend. Many offer afternoon tea, and all their goodies are usually homemade.

Get Connected

- To search for a bed-and-breakfast, check out *bbonline.com.*

- To search for a teahouse in your area, try *teamap.com.*

- Key search words: high tea or afternoon tea followed by your city and state, teahouse, tearoom recipes

Love is love's reward.

JOHN DRYDEN

39. Sing Your Hearts Out

A date for karaoke is not for the fainthearted. It's probable that you will hear some truly disturbing performances of some of your favorite songs. But that's part of the fun. Plus, it leaves you thinking positively about your own rendition of the Righteous Brothers' "Unchained Melody" or Carrie Underwood's "Jesus, Take the Wheel" or—well . . . you decide.

Karaoke can be found all over town these days. All you have to do is take a number and your place in the audience. Opt for beverages without ice to preserve your voice timbre. (That's what the pros do.) When it's your turn, try a duet. The words will be projected on a screen in front of you, so no worries. Just sing your little hearts out—and then laugh until you think you'll drop. Beware. Some couples have had so much fun on this date that they have caught the "entertainment bug," returning week after week for the lights, the music, and the applause.

Budget

$$ You'll need to cover beverages and finger food or perhaps dinner. Some places have a cover charge.

 **Over the Top**

- Purchase a favorite CD and rehearse your performance at home.

- Buy karaoke equipment and have your own karaoke parties at home.

 Get Connected

Key search words: karaoke followed by your city and state, karaoke machine

40. Day at the Spa

Imagine for a moment the two of you lying facedown on side-by-side massage tables, holding hands across the distance in between. Soothing music is playing. Oils are burning nearby, releasing exotic fragrances into the air, while massage therapists bring relief to stressed muscles and push the tension from your bodies. Now that's a date! And when the massages are over, spas have many other luxuries in which to indulge, like skin treatments for both men and women, healthy lunches, and much more.

You can book a full day or just a lazy afternoon. Whatever you choose, it will keep you thinking beautiful thoughts about each other for a long time to come.

 Budget

$$$ Spa dates can be pricey, so you will want to save up for this one. Your best bet is to look for specials on sweetheart packages.

 Steps to Success

- Book early to get the best package and the dates you prefer.

- Friday afternoons are ideal. You have the weekend to relax.

- Turn off your cell phones.

- Agree that there will be no talking about work or challenges at home.

Over the Top

Book a full weekend and take advantage of all the spa has to offer.

Get Connected

Key search words: spa or spa packages followed by your city and state

41. O Christmas Tree!

Head to a nearby Christmas tree lot or farm to pick out the perfect Christmas tree. Then enjoy an evening of listening to Christmas carols and decorating the tree. If this is an activity you traditionally share with the kids, keep up your tradition, and then plan some special alone time for the two of you after the kids go to bed. Snuggle up and enjoy some holiday treats as you admire your newly decorated tree.

Purchase or make a special ornament for the two of you to hang on the tree after the children are in bed—one that has something to do with your unique love story. You could even plan to exchange small pre-Christmas gifts, the first to go under the tree. Share memories of your best Christmases together, watch your favorite Christmas movie, or bake a Christmas goody together.

Budget

$-$$$ You'll need to plan for enough money to purchase your tree, perhaps a new ornament, and maybe some special holiday goodies.

Over the Top

- Choose a tree in your yard and decorate it together.

- Pick out a small tree to set up in your bedroom and decorate it with romantic, sentimental items. You could even pull out old love notes and Christmas cards you've given to each other and use them to decorate the tree.

Get Connected

Key search words: Christmas trees, Christmas movies, Christmas ornaments, Christmas recipes

A Kiss

And what is a kiss, when all is done?

A promise given under seal—a vow

A signature acknowledged—a rosy dot

Over the i of Loving—a secret whispered

To listening lips apart—a moment made

Immortal, with a rush of wings unseen—

A sacrament of blossoms, a new song

Sung by two hearts to an old simple tune—

The ring of one horizon around two souls

Together, all alone!

EDMOND ROSTAND

42. Croquet on the Lawn

Croquet, better known in England than in the USA, is a sport known for its advanced gentility. Football and hockey devotees will find it remarkably docile. But some might argue that cut-throat competition

and groveling in the dirt are not well suited to the civilities of dating.

Consider for a moment the bevy of benefits croquet can offer: (1) brisk exercise, (2) the challenge of conquering a sport played by kings and queens, (3) an opportunity to become familiar with mallets, and (4) one of the few sports you can actually engage in while carrying on a credible conversation. Not bad!

Set up your croquet set on the lawn and make a date for a big play-off to be held on the next sunny afternoon at home. Up the stakes a bit by declaring that the loser buys the winner an ice-cream sundae.

Budget

$-$$ You probably already have a croquet set—no? Then you will have to purchase one.

Steps to Success

- Sports equipment stores usually sell croquet sets.

- If you don't have a yard, set up at a local park.

Over the Top

Dress up for the big game. Women should wear a dress, loose fitting and of a light, airy fabric. Men should wear knickers, and bow ties are encouraged.

Get Connected

Key search words: new croquet set, used croquet set, history of croquet

43. All Aboard!

Passenger trains aren't as easily accessible as they used to be, but if you have a historic, scenic railroad nearby, you have the makings of a charming and greatly enjoyable date. Short-run scenic trains usually provide opportunities to view splendid autumn colors, breathtaking landscapes, and snow scenes from observation cars with full-length windows and glass ceilings. Many include dinner. And some provide entertainment—singers, musicians, or even interactive role playing. In some areas, you can climb aboard a Christmas train for a special treat. These include a holiday dinner, Christmas carol sing-alongs, and many other holiday surprises.

No doubt about it, an excursion train trip can be that special date you are looking for and one which will engender many fond memories.

Budget

$$-$$$ Cost for excursion trains vary widely, depending on the length of the trip and the extras offered.

Steps to Success

- Book early, especially around the holidays.

- Dress comfortably. Layers are best since

temperatures inside the cars vary widely—some are cold and drafty, others warm and stuffy.

- Wear sunglasses. Glare in observation cars can be intense.

- Turn off your cell phone.

- For longer rides, take along something to read.

- Don't forget your camera.

WOW **Over the Top**

Take a train trip vacation, enjoying all the scenery you might not see by car. Imagine snuggling together in your compartment as you watch the sun set outside your window.

Get Connected

- You can find a directory of scenic railroads listed by state at *railsusa.com*.

- Check out *amtrak.com* for vacation packages.

- Key search words: train vacation packages, dinner trains

In the eyes of a lover pockmarks are dimples.

JAPANESE PROVERB

44. Jumbo Boxing

This date is strictly for laughs and guaranteed to leave you breathless and doubled over. Try it once when you are alone, and then invite friends over for some extra rounds. Like its sister sport "sumo wrestling," jumbo boxing requires the use of oversized gloves made from high density foam or inflated with air.

Mark off an area of play from which the two of you cannot stray, except during breaks. Set down some ground rules: No kicking, tripping, pushing, or biting. Taunting in jest is encouraged. Two-minute rounds. Loser cooks dinner.

If you feel like sharing the fun, invite a few friends to referee and videotape the event. Give all the other couples an opportunity to don the gloves and take each other to the mat.

Budget

$$-$$$ You'll need to buy or rent gloves, headgear, and a mat.

Steps to Success

- Make sure you're boxing on a mat or a soft surface.

- Wear shoes.

- Use an egg timer to time the rounds.

- Music helps.

- Rules are the same as regular boxing.

- Quit the second it stops being fun and starts feeling like a fight.

Over the Top

Rent a giant, bouncy boxing ring with the gloves and gear included. Set it up in the backyard; assign trainers, referees, and judges; and invite spectators. Play the theme to *Rocky* during the matches.

Get Connected

- Check out *ebay.com* for used gloves, headgear, and a mat.

- Key search words: jumbo boxing gear and equipment

45. Hop on a Motorcycle

If you own a motorcycle, you already know what it's like to feel the engine below you, your sweetheart's arms hugging you from behind, and the wind rushing past you at fifty miles per hour. It's a

kick! And for those who don't have a bike of their own, look into a rental.

Inexperienced riders should stay away from freeways. Stick to local streets and familiar local highways and hold down your speed! Choose a destination before you leave, and plan to keep your trip under an hour. Take along a couple of sandwiches and sodas to share at some pretty place along the route.

 **Budget**

$$$ Due to high insurance rates, motorcycle rentals can be more pricey than a car rental.

Steps to Success

- Ask the rental agent to go over all the technical stuff with you. Riding a motorcycle is only slightly the same as driving a car.

- Watch for hot pipes when getting on and off the motorcycle.

- Observe all traffic signs and the rules governing driving a car.

- Layer your clothes.

- Cover your arms and legs.

- Make sure to wear a helmet!

Get Connected

Key search words: motorcycle rental

Romance Him

Even if you hate sports,
choose a game your husband is
particularly interested in and watch it
with him. Sit as close to him as possible,
but don't ask a lot of questions (men hate
that). Simply cheer enthusiastically when he
does, express indignation when he does,
and share a crestfallen moment when
his team is down and out. He'll
love that you are giving him
and his team your undivided
attention.

46. Dinner on Deck

From San Diego to Seattle, Florida to New York, to the full length of the Gulf Coast and along the Great Lakes, you can find the very special dining experience known as a dinner cruise. And for those who live inland, there are riverboats. This is truly a great choice for those big-ticket dates celebrating birthdays, anniversaries, and gutsy career moves.

As if eating a romantic meal on board were not enough, almost all these cruises include dancing, Vegas-style floor shows, and various other attractions. Most will take a picture of the two of you on your special night for your scrapbook.

 **Budget**

$$$ These grand evenings on the water don't come cheap. However, public cruises are more affordable than private outings.

What to Take

- Your informational brochure will tell you what to wear. Some are quite formal; others (such as sailboat cruises in the Gulf of Mexico) ask for vacation wear, such as sundresses and casual pants and shirts.

- Sunglasses. Until the sun goes down, the glare off the water can be intense.

- Sunscreen

- A light jacket. Even in warm weather,

breezes on the water can be cool.

- Motion sickness medication. Check the label carefully because some will make you drowsy.

- Reasonable heels. Walking on the deck of a moving vessel is not like walking on terra firma.

Steps to Success

Cruises should be booked as far in advance as possible.

Get Connected

Key search words: dinner cruise, riverboat cruise, sailboat cruise followed by your city and state

47. Scuba Lessons

Amazing colors in all hues of the rainbow, some almost neon. That is what you'll see when scuba diving. It's an amazing sport! Some swear by it. Others find they are not well suited to endure the water pressure and breathing techniques. A few even suffer from panic attacks. Regardless of what you ultimately decide on the matter, the lessons can be an exciting trial run for the two of you.

Initially you will spend time in a classroom learning about the sport and how to manage yourself and your gear underwater. Then you move on to a trial swim, fully suited up in a tank. If you pass that milestone and wish to continue, your instructor will invite you to go along on a scuba trip, where you can get more supervised experience. Even if you drop out after the classroom sessions, you will have had a unique and fascinating experience. And who knows, the two of you might turn out to be real scuba enthusiasts.

 **Budget**

$$-$$$ Lessons are reasonably priced—but the gear is another story. It's best to rent gear until you decide if this sport is for you.

Steps to Success

Six questions you should ask yourself before
signing up

- What is the age requirement?

- Do I need to be physically fit?

- Do I have to be able to swim?

- How do I choose an instructor?

- How long is the course and how much
does it cost?

- What other skills can we learn?

Get Connected

- Find the answer to these questions at
scuba.about.com.

- Key search words: scuba lessons followed
by your city and state

48. You Pick!

If you haven't done this before, you'll be amazed at
how much fun it is. Make a date to go together to
a local orchard or berry farm. Choose something
you both really like to eat and be sure to plan

carefully. What you take home will have to be dealt with—canned, frozen, served, or given away within a few days or a week at most.

In many parts of the country, you will be able to pick apples, peaches, pears, strawberries, blueberries, blackberries, cherries, maybe even figs. In some areas your choices are even broader.

If you aren't feeling up to doing the work yourself, you can buy what you want—already picked by someone else! Most farms also carry jams and jellies, honey, derivative items, juices, and a variety of other fascinating products. You'll go home with smiles on your faces and your arms full of the earth's bounty.

Budget

$-$$ Cost is reasonable, even if you don't choose to pick the fruit yourself.

What to Take

- Gardening gloves
- Long-sleeved tops and long pants
- Hat
- Comfortable shoes
- Insect repellent

Get Connected

Key search words: pick your own black-berries (or whatever fruit you want) followed by your city and state

49. Visit Your Alma Mater

College is a special time. For most it's the first experience away from home, a pivotal chance to explore your boundaries and define yourself. Going back together will give you an opportunity to see each other through brand-new eyes.

If you met in college, you are ahead of the game. Go back and visit all those places of significance—the place where you met, where you shared your first kiss or declared your love for each other. If you went to different schools, take your spouse by the hand and visit both campuses. Give each other a deluxe, private tour, complete with all your cherished memories, hilarious moments, and those events that made you the person your spouse fell in love with.

If distance prevents you from visiting in person, get out the yearbooks and spend a quiet evening walking through them page by page. You might be surprised to find so many loving memories suddenly popping to the surface.

 Budget

> $$-$$$ A visit to your campus or campuses could be costly if you no longer live in the area. If you are on a tight budget, a quiet

evening at home with a yearbook can also be fun. But you will want to arrange for dinner and a sitter.

What to Take

- A yearbook is a great reference for names of people you'll want to reconnect with.

- Visit the Alumni Center and get a current map of the campus, along with identification badges, which are often needed with more stringent security measures in place.

Over the Top

Attend a college reunion. Before you go, try to contact some of your old friends who will be attending and plan to hang out together.

Get Connected

Key search words: name of alma mater, hotel followed by the name of the town where the school is located, find college friend

Love
consists in desiring
to give what is our own to
another and feeling his
delight as our own.

EMANUEL SWEDENBORG

My Love, My Life

What greater thing is there for two
   human souls

than to feel that they are joined for life,

to strengthen each other in all labor,

to rest on each other in all sorrow,

to minister to each other in all pain,

to be one with each other

in silent, unspeakable memories at the
   moment of the last parting.

GEORGE ELIOT

50. Carriage Ride

Step back in time and enjoy the charm and romance of a horse-drawn carriage ride. These rides are often offered in downtown areas or in historic districts. They can be arranged ahead of time or are usually available as a spur-of-the-moment idea, perhaps as the crowning jewel to a nice dinner out. The drivers will many times have interesting tidbits to share about the surrounding area along the way. Snuggle up, enjoy the scenery, and imagine yourselves in a different time.

Budget

$$ Prices will vary depending on location, but most horse-drawn carriage rides are reasonable for something to do that is out of the ordinary.

Over the Top

- If you live in an area that gets heavy snow-falls, an old-fashioned horse-drawn sleigh ride is a romantic wintertime diversion.

- For a more adventurous date, skip the carriage and get right on the horse! Horse-back riding can be a fun experience, even for beginners. Some stables even offer special packages that include a campfire dinner or cattle-drive experience.

- Visit New York City during the Christmas holidays. Take a carriage ride through Central Park.

Get Connected

Key search words: horse-drawn carriage rides, horse-drawn sleigh rides, horseback riding

The most precious possession that ever comes to a man in this world is a woman's heart.

JOSIAH G. HOLLAND

51. Your Dream Neighborhood

Is there an area of town you like to drive through just to admire the beautiful homes? Why not take that to the next level on some pleasant weekend afternoon by attending an open house or two so you can take a peek inside?

Take your time and enjoy fantasizing about what it would be like to live in the house. Explore the layout and point out the details. Take a small notepad along to jot down features you would like to have in your dream home one day. As you

admire the fine workmanship and artful landscaping,
you'll have a good time together as well as estab-
lishing a dream for the two of you to work toward.

 **Budget**

$ One great thing about attending open
houses is that it won't cost you a dime!

Over the Top

- If this is an activity you both really enjoy,
consider finding out when there will be a
Parade of Homes in your area and plan to
attend.

- After you go to some open houses, plan a
renovation project in your own home to
include some of the features you liked from
the houses you looked at.

Get Connected

Key search words: open house, parade of homes followed by your city and state

If love were what the rose is,

And I were like the leaf,

Our lives would grow together

In sad or singing weather.

ALGERNON CHARLES SWINBURNE

52. Retro Date

You love to dress up, so why not make a night of it?
You can choose any decade you like—poodle skirts
and greasy hair for the '50s, big hair and penny
loafers for the '60s, Afros and leisure suits for the

'70s. You get the picture. And don't worry about other people's reactions if you go out on the town. You will inspirc thcm to do the same or at least cause them to smile.

After you choose a decade, plan your date around that era. Dress up in the trendy outfits of the day, and don't forget to re-create those fabulous hair styles. Dance to that decade's greatest hits. Watch a classic movie or a TV series from that decade. (Many stores now sell classic series on DVD.) Be sure to eat the foods specific to your era too. (For example, if you choose the '50s, eat TV dinners or a homemade tuna casserole at home, or eat at an old-time diner.) Give each other a pop culture quiz. Make out in the backseat of your car!

Before the night is over, be sure to take pictures. You'll want to remember this date for many years.

 **Budget**

$-$$ You can save a lot of money on costumes by shopping at thrift stores. You can usually rent classic TV series or movies if you don't want to buy them. And making your own retro meal can save you money.

 Steps to Success

- Sit down first and brainstorm. Choose your

target decade by secret ballot so you both get to see the other's first choice. If your choices differ, you may have to make this a two-date affair.

- Shop for costumes, movies, music, and food together. Make this prep time part of the date.

Over the Top

Host a retro party. Enlist the help of friends for planning and preparation.

Get Connected

- If you opt for a '50s night, check out *fiftiesweb.com*.

- Key search words: retro party, '50s themed party, '60s music, food in '70s, '50s food recipes

Also look for this book:

HOWARD BOOKS
A DIVISION OF SIMON & SCHUSTER
New York   London   Toronto   Sydney